Learn to Play the Highland Bagpipe

Recommended by some of the world`s greatest pipers

Publisher

"printed and published by BoD - Books on Demand, Norderstedt"

BOD – Books on Demand GmbH
ISBN 978-3-75-198537-6

2th Edition 2020
English

Web
www.bagpipe-shop.com

E-mail
info@bagpiper-andy.de

Cover/Photos – Heidi Mayer/Andreas Hambsch
Contents/Text – Andreas Hambsch

Table of Contents

Description of the book

What you'll need in addition to this book

1) An A4-sized music book with empty staffs (note lines). You'll write your exercises in your music book *and especially* the tunes you'll learn, because physically writing them down is really an *enormous* help for the learning process.

2) During your first year of learning, you'll also need a practice chanter. You can find one in any specialised shop for bagpipes and accessories. The staff there will be able to give you the special advice you need. If you have a tutor, ask him or her to recommend a practice chanter and accessories.

You'll learn the first fingerings and tunes on your practice chanter and after around 8-16 months (depending on the time you spend on the exercises), you'll have reached lesson 21. Then it will be time for you to transfer what you've learned on your chanter to the "big" bagpipes – but the practice chanter will always accompany you when you're learning fingering exercises and new tunes.

The Structure of the Book

Bagpipe music has melody notes (they're the big notes, which represent the melody of the tune) and grace notes (the small notes), which "grace" or embellish the melody.
With this method and twenty-eight lessons, this book is structured in such a way that you can absorb and memorise the melody and grace notes systematically and successfully.

The **Bagpipe Tutorial App** contains the acoustic and visual versions of all the exercises in this book, plus all tunes played at different speeds. **You can download the app in your app store**.

Each lesson in the book will bring you one step closer to your goal of becoming a good piper. Work through the lessons conscientiously – only start the next one if you're sure you've mastered the previous lesson's exercises and can play them correctly.

By the time you've finished with this book, you'll have learned twenty-two bagpipe tunes (yes, twenty-two!) with all their grace notes. But keep working on your fingering technique every day – and expand your repertoire using sheet music that you can buy in your bagpipe shop.

This textbook is suitable for studying without a teacher, but it's also the ideal companion book if you are taking private lessons.

In Lesson 28 you'll find a summary of all the exercises in the chapters, plus the embellishments of classical music (Piobaireachd).

About the Bagpipe Tutorial App: Recommended by the best pipers in the world!

This tutorial app is the most comprehensive multimedia reference in the world on playing the Scottish bagpipes. It contains more than 250 videos demonstrating control of the instrument and finger techniques, including audio-visual information on all the grace notes and embellishments. Numerous exercises convey the essentials of Scottish piping.

Info: For each download of the *full version*, a part of the revenue flows into a social project, which will be announced by Andreas Hambsch on Facebook at the end of the year.

Info: To receive vouchers and interesting information about bagpipes, activate push notifications in the settings of your mobile phone.
(Only with the full version)

Once the app is installed, you have access to all of its functions and all the videos, even in offline mode. The tutorial is ideal for absolute beginners up to advanced pipers and can be used for independent study or as a source of examples for lessons. Its aim is to give the student basic information about the instrument, a solid foundation in technique and expert guidance on the route to becoming an accomplished piper.

This tutorial app by Andreas Hambsch is a milestone in the teaching of the Scottish bagpipes. Easily understandable and thorough, it is a worthwhile investment for anyone interested in piping. The Bagpipe Tutorial book, also by Andreas Hambsch, is an ideal supplement.

Lesson 1 – Fingering on the Practice Chanter

"App – Videos – Basic Exercises 1 – Fingering on the Practice Chanter"

Look at these pictures to see how your fingers should be placed on the practice chanter. It's usual practice to have your left hand above your right, but some students find it easier the other way around – and if right above left is more comfortable for you, no problem! Start by placing your right hand fingers on the lower four fingerholes.

1. Right hand – place the upper pad of your pinkie on the lowest fingerhole **(Low A finger)**.

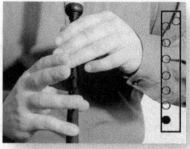

2. Right hand – place the middle pad of your ring finger over the second lowest fingerhole **(B finger)**.

3. Right hand – place the middle pad of your middle finger over the third lowest fingerhole **(C finger).**

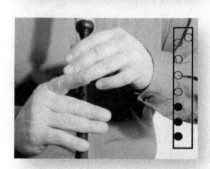

4. Right hand – place the middle pad of your index finger over the fourth lowest fingerhole **(D finger).**

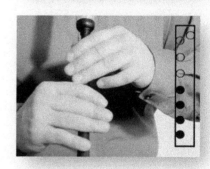

Your right thumb should be positioned on the back of the chanter at a height between the index and middle fingers – apply only light pressure.

OK, your lower (right) hand is on the chanter, now let's position the left hand.

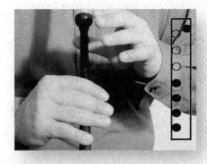

5. Left hand – place your thumb on the rear fingerhole **(High A finger)**.

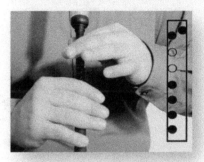

6. Left hand – place the upper or middle pad of your index finger on the highest fingerhole **(High G finger).**

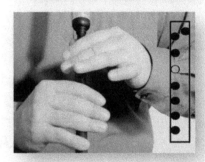

7. Left hand – place the upper or middle pad of your middle finger on the next fingerhole **(F finger)**.

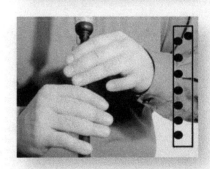

8. Left hand – place the upper pad of your ring finger on the next fingerhole **(E finger)**.

Remember...
Use only gentle pressure on the chanter with your upper and lower thumbs.
All your fingers should be lying straight (stretched but relaxed) on the chanter.

Take your fingers off the chanter and put them back on again – repeat this process several times to get into the right routine.

A mirror is a great help for checking your fingers to see if they are lying straight and correctly on the chanter.

The fingering chart below will help you with the second lesson.

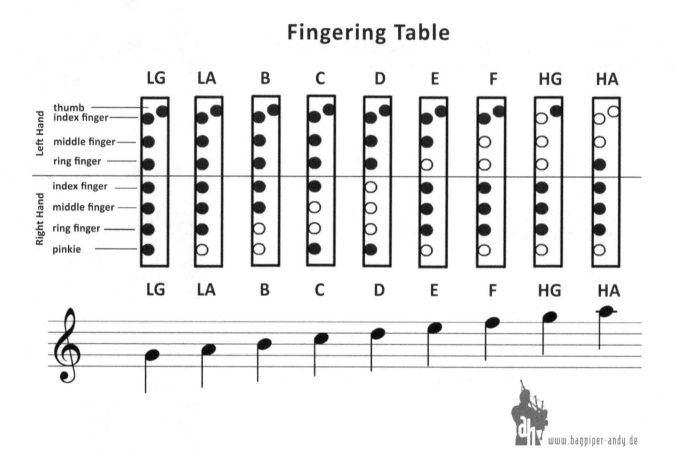

www.bagpiper-andy.de

Remember...

While you're learning the following lessons, NEVER write the names (letters) of the notes under the exercises (tunes). When you see a note, you must know how to finger it without even having to *think* about its name.

Lesson 2 – Scales and Exercises

The first note – Low G

Place all your fingers on the chanter as described. Now blow gently into the mouthpiece. The note you're now hearing is the first and lowest note, the

Low G

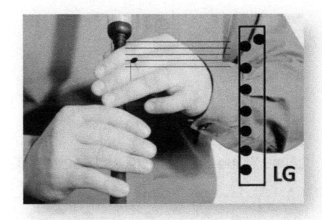

The second note – Low A

Now lift your lower pinkie and blow gently again. This is the

Low A

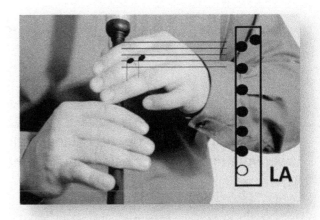

Low G to Low A Scale

"App – Videos – Basic Exercises 1 – Low G to Low A Scale"

Play this exercise a few times, making sure that your fingers are lying straight (stretched but relaxed) on the chanter.

Remember...
Play the notes slowly and evenly.

The third note – B

Now lift your right (hand) ring finger to play the next note. Blow gently into the chanter again.
This is a

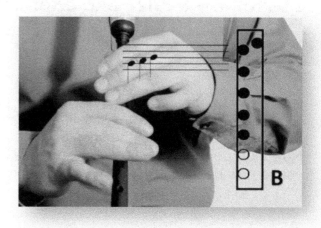

Low G to B Scale

"App – Videos – Basic Exercises 1 – Low G to B Scale"

Play this scale a few times until you're confident your fingering is correct.

The fourth note – C

Lift your right middle finger and at the same time, lower your right pinkie, closing that fingerhole.
This is a

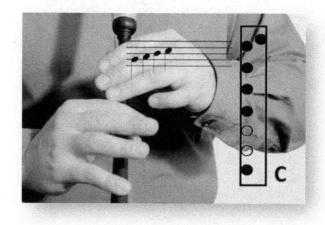

Low G to C Scale

"App – Videos – Basic Exercises 1 – Low G to C Scale"

Play this exercise a few times until the fingering is no problem for you. Make sure the notes sound clean when you're changing fingers.

Low G to C Exercise
"App – Videos – Basic Exercises 1 – Low G to C Exercise"

The fifth note – D
Now lift your right index finger as well, but keep your pinkie on its fingerhole.

This is a

D

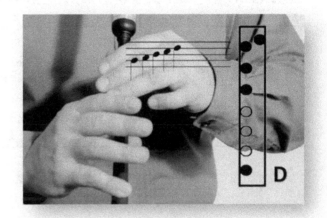

Low G to D Scale
"App – Videos – Basic Exercises 1 – Low G to D Scale"

Low G to D Exercise
"App – Videos – Basic Exercises 1 – Low G to D Exercise"

The sixth note – E
Now it's time to change hands! To do this, place the ring, middle and index fingers of your right hand on their respective fingerholes.

At the same time, lift the ring finger of your left hand and the pinkie of your right hand.

This is an

E

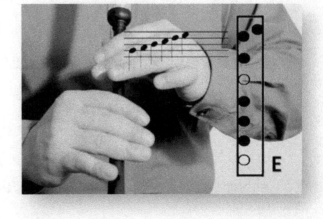

Low G to E Scale
"App – Videos – Basic Exercises 1 – Low G to E Scale"

Low G to E Exercise & D to E Exercise
"App – Videos – Basic Exercises 1 – Low G to E Exercise"

"App – Videos – Basic Exercises 1 – D to E Exercise"

Play these three exercises several times through. Make sure your hand changes are clean. When you're changing notes, try to avoid "crossing noises". Crossing noises are small sounds that are heard when you change notes.

The seventh note – F
Lift your left middle finger to get to the next note.
Leave your lower hand as is on the chanter.
This is an

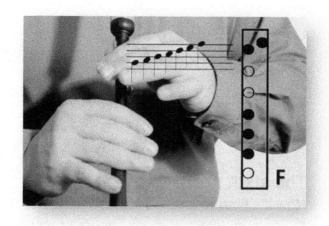

Low G to F Scale
"App – Videos – Basic Exercises 1 – Low G to F Scale"

You should only continue with the next exercise when you can play all the previous ones accurately.

13

Low G to F Exercise
"App – Videos – Basic Exercises 1 – Low G to F Exercise"

The eighth note – High G

Lift your left index finger. Make sure that your left index, middle and ring fingers don't stray too far up from the chanter. This is a

High G

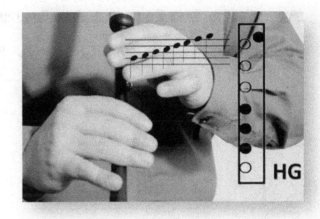

Low G to High G Scale
"App – Videos – Basic Exercises 1 – Low G to High G Scale"

Low G to High G Exercise
"App – Videos – Basic Exercises 1 – Low G to High G Exercise"

The ninth note – High A

Now lower your left ring finger back on to the fingerhole and lift your left thumb at the same time. This is the

High A

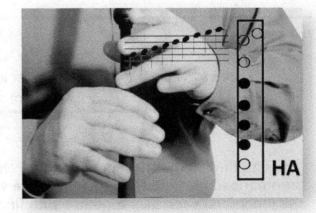

Low G to High A Scale (Complete Scale)
"App – Videos – Basic Exercises 1 – Low G to High A Scale"

Low G to High A Exercise
"App – Videos – Basic Exercises 1 – Low G to High A Exercise"

E to High A exercise

High G to High A exercise

Write down *all* the exercises you've learned in your music book. Always start by drawing the bar lines to divide the space in the staff correctly.

Practise the finger exercises you've learned slowly and smoothly. Set a metronome at slow speed to help you and play one melody note per beat.

Only go on to the next page if you're confident that you can play all the exercises correctly.

Remember...
From now on, NO LOOKING AT YOUR FINGERS!
Always hold the practice chanter loosely in your fingers – don't tighten up!
And practise every day!

You can find all these grace notes, the embellishments and the most important exercises summarised in lesson 28. This will save you a lot of page turning when you're performing the individual exercises together with finger technique exercises.

Play the following note **change exercises** as often as you can for several days – and focus on what you've learned. When you're sure you've mastered the exercises, you can start **lesson 3**.

"App – Videos – Basic Exercises 2 – Changing Exercise 1 - 7"

First play all the notes on the lines.

Now play the notes in the spaces between the lines.

This is the "big jumps" exercise. Change fingers cleanly, avoiding "crossing noises".

Does this tune sound familiar?

Play all the notes on the lines again.

Change notes cleanly!

This exercise helps your fingers to move precisely.

Congratulations! Now you've learned the complete scale and some important exercises too! You've reached the first milestone on your journey to becoming a good bagpipe player!

Lesson 3 – Music Theory

Now it's time to learn some basic theoretical knowledge about music.

The Clef

The clef is always placed at the beginning of the lines of notes (called the staff). As far as we pipers are concerned, its only function is to show us the line where the Low G is, otherwise it's not so important for us.
Try drawing it a few times in your music book.

The Repeat Signs

 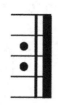

In some song music, you'll find these at the beginning and at the end of a part. As the name suggests, the repeat signs mean you should play the lines within the signs twice in succession.

The Bar

A bar goes from one vertical line to the next one. A song part often consists of eight bars on two note lines. **Two bars = one phrase**.

The Time Signature

The time signature tells us the note value in a bar and how many beats are in that bar. With a 2/4 time signature, you have two quarter notes, each with one beat (however, a quarter note can also be represented by notes of different values, e.g. two eighth notes, four sixteenth notes and so on).

A Dotted Note

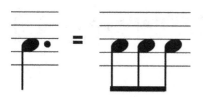

A dot behind a note tells us that it must be extended by half of its value. So a dotted quarter note would have a length of one quarter note + half of one quarter note (=one eighth note), amounting to three eighth notes altogether.

Melody and Grace Notes

We differentiate between **melody notes** and **grace notes**. Melody notes are the bigger notes. Their stems always point downwards and are attached to the left of the note head. Melody notes give us the melody of a bagpipe tune. In contrast, grace notes are the smaller notes – their stems always point upwards and are attached to the right of the note head. These notes are also called embellishments. They grace (embellish, decorate) a melody. We can use a grace note to separate two identical melody notes or to play a transition from one note to the next. A combination of several of these grace notes is called an **embellishment or movement**.

A whole note has the length of two half notes. A half note has the length of two quarter notes. A quarter note has the length of two eighth notes. An eighth note has the length of two sixteenth notes. A sixteenth note has the length of two thirty-second notes (see below).

Remember...

The time interval of the beats tells you the speed of the song. The speed is relative, since each song and each exercise can *and should* be played at different speeds.

If you practise slowly and play cleanly you'll become a better piper!

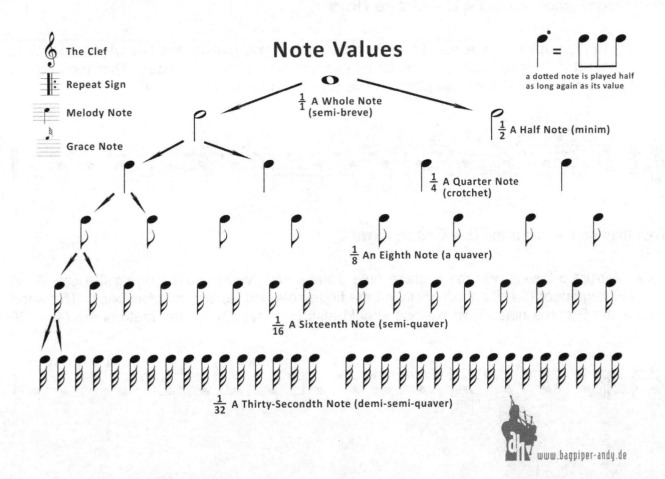

Now you've gained an insight into the theory of music. If you have any questions, talk to your teacher about this and ask him or her to explain the details using examples. The best way to learn how to "keep the beat" and learn the characteristics of rhythm is by using a metronome.

Now we come to **lesson 4**, which covers the single and fundamental grace notes.

Lesson 4 – Single Grace Notes

Your first grace note is the **High G – Grace Note**

Try to interrupt a Low A using the G grace note. I can almost hear you saying "What?" Don't worry, it's easy. Here's how to do it – as you play the Low A, lift your left index finger (the High G finger) briefly off the fingerhole and replace it immediately (a fast off-on move). This short note is the G grace note. Try playing the following exercise with the metronome (40 - 60 bpm) and play a grace note on each beat.

Your second grace note is the **D – Grace Note**

Now try to interrupt a Low A using the D grace note. While playing the Low A, lift your right index finger (the D finger) briefly off the fingerhole and replace it immediately. This short note is the D grace note. You should also play this exercise using the metronome (40 – 60 bpm).

Your third grace note is the **E – Grace Note**

Let's interrupt a Low A with the E grace note. Here's how: while you're playing the Low A, lift your left ring finger (the E finger) briefly off the fingerhole and replace it immediately. This short note is the E grace note. This exercise should also be played using the metronome (40 – 60 bpm).

Now write down the first **grace note exercises** in your music book.

Practise these first grace note exercises for a while, until you're playing all three grace notes at the same even speed. Try to always play your grace notes exactly on each beat of the metronome or the tapping of your foot.

Remember...
Always play the grace notes at a slow and steady speed.
Lift all the fingers with which you play the grace notes to the same height (about 2.5 cm).

Now we'll learn how to play the "G-D-E grace notes" in that order. Work as hard as you possibly can on the next exercises (but don't forget to eat and drink!).

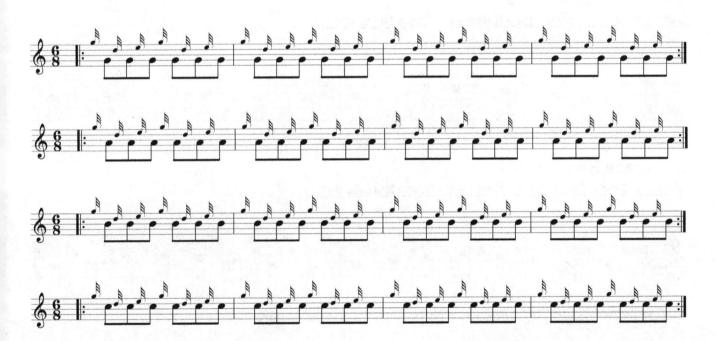

Now write down the **"G-D-E grace note"** exercises in your music book.

When you've mastered these finger exercises, you can try playing note changes with a grace note in the next lesson.

Lesson 5 – Changing Notes with a Grace Note

Here's how changing notes with a grace note works – let's say you're on a melody note and you open a grace note. While you're closing your grace note again, you switch to the next melody note.

To help you grasp this and get it right, let's try to play the grace note scales.

High G – Grace Note Scale
"App – Videos – Single Grace Notes – High G - Grace Note Scale"

D – Grace Note Scale
"App – Videos – Single Grace Notes – D - Grace Note Scale"

E – Grace Note Scale
"App – Videos – Single Grace Notes – E - Grace Note Scale"

Now write down the **"Single Grace Note"** scales in your music book.

Remember...
Try to set the beat on each grace note with your foot or the metronome.

Now let's move on to more note change exercises combined with the G-D-E grace notes. Practise the following lines as carefully and as regularly as you can. Start the next lesson _only_ if you're sure you can play the previous exercises cleanly and if you know that your timing of the grace notes is just fine.

21

G-D-E Exercise:

These finger exercises are also important for experienced pipers!

How far off the chanter should you raise your fingers when you play the grace notes?

"App – Videos – Single Grace Notes – G-D-E Exercise 1 - 5"

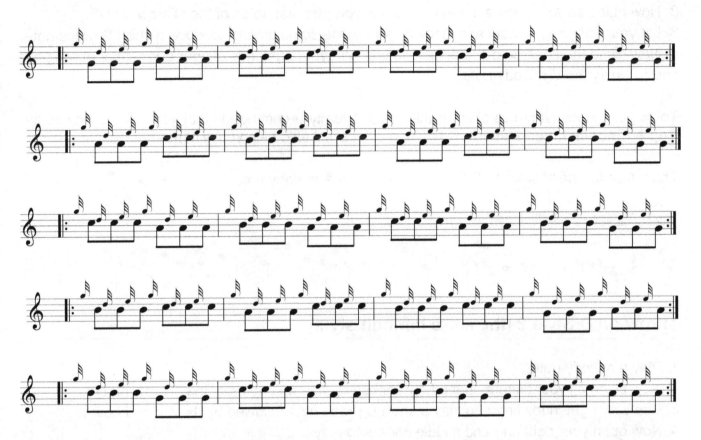

Now write down the **"G-D-E Exercise"** scales in your music book.

Remember...
In the above exercises, always try to play the G grace note on the beat of the bar and keep time with it. The metronome can help you with this.

Do you know the names of your fingers already?

right pinkie?   *right ring finger?*   *right middle finger?*

right index finger?   *left ring finger?*   *left middle finger?*

left index finger?   *left thumb?*

Lesson 6 – "Throw on D" and your First Tune

Now you're ready to learn the first complex embellishment – the **"Throw on D"**. There are two different playing styles for the Throw on D – you can choose the one you like best.

Throw on D Style 1 (the most common style and the simplest)

1. Play a melody note.
2. Now place all your fingers in the Low G position (the first notes of the "Throw on D").
3. Lift your right ring, middle and index fingers at the same time to produce a short D grace note.
4. Now close the fingerhole immediately again with your right index finger and – after playing a short C, play the D melody note.

To avoid unnecessary mistakes at this point, I really recommend that you take a look in the **App`s Embellishments section**. The app videos will also help you with the next lesson.

The music for the "Throw on D Style 1" of the Low A melody note:

"App – Videos – Embellishments – Throw on D Style 1"

Throw on D Style 2 (the more difficult style)

1. Play a melody note.
2. Now place all your fingers on the Low G position (the first notes of the "Throw on D").
3. Use your right index finger to play a short D grace note followed by the second Low G.
4. Now open your right ring and middle fingers to play a C.
5. Now raise your right index finger to play a melody note D.

The music for the "Throw on D Style 2" of the Low A melody note:

"App – Videos – Embellishments – Throw on D Style 2"

Remember...
Style 1 is used in most sheet music collections. Now that you've learned style 2, always play it instead of style 1.

Now write down both of the **"Throw on D"** scales in your music book.

Congratulations! Now you've learned the basics – and it's time to start learning your first **"tune"** for the pipes. It's a "Slow Air" (a slow, stately tune) in 6/8 called **"Scots Wha Ha'e"**. This tune is one of the unofficial national anthems of Scotland. Let's take a look at the first part.
There's a grace note on the Low G line in the bar before last. Play it as follows: the melody note B, a short Low G and the eighth melody note Low A.

Scots Wha Ha'e "Part 1"   **Slow Air**   **traditional**
"App – Videos – Bagpipe Tutorial Tunes"

Now write down the **"first part"** of this tune in your music book.

Listen to the melody on the **app videos** several times and try to play it right through every day – slowly and cleanly. Can you play the first half of the tune easily and smoothly? Honestly? OK, you're ready for the next lesson!

Lesson 7 – Half Strikes and Double High G

You're going to need two more embellishments for the second part of "Scots Wha Ha'e" –
the "Half Strike" and the "Double High G"

Half Strikes

First play the melody notes and close briefly to play the short thirty-second note. The difference between a grace note and a half strike is that for a grace note a fingerhole is opened briefly, but one or more holes are briefly closed for a half strike.

"App – Videos – Embellishments – Half Strikes"

Now write down the **"Half Strike"** exercise in your music book.

Double High G

For the Double High G, first play a melody note. Now open all the fingers of the upper left hand (except the thumb) on the G grace note, play a short F with your left index finger and use the same finger to return to the High G melody note. Pay attention to your right hand here! (from High A melody note, you only play a short F to the High G)

The music for the Double High G from the Low A melody note:

"App – Videos – Doublings – Double High G"

Now write down the **"Double High G"** scale in your music book.

Play the exercises a few times through until you're confident in your finger movements. Now you can try the second part of Scots Wha Ha'e.

Scots Wha Ha'e "Part 2"   traditional

"App – Videos – Bagpipe Tutorial Tunes"

Now write down the **"second part"** of this tune in your music book.

Copying exercises and tunes into your music book has a very important learning effect on your memory. OK, it might be a tiresome task for some of you – but I really can't emphasise enough just how important it is.

When you write down the melody notes, grace notes and embellishments, you automatically become very aware of what you have to play. Your understanding of the notes is enhanced and with time you'll develop a good grasp of how the combinations of notes are composed.

And it even helps your memorising process!

Scots Wha Ha'e "Parts 1 and 2"   Slow Air   traditional
"App – Videos – Bagpipe Tutorial Tunes"

Scots Wha Ha'e is written in 6/8 time. Practice the 6/8 by keeping the beat on each eighth note. This will help you to create the right rhythm for the tune. Use the **app videos** while you're learning and listen to the tune as often as possible.

An eighth note consists of one beat. A quarter note consists of two beats. A dotted quarter note consists of three beats **(See lesson 3)**.

When you can play the tune well, switch to two beats per bar. One beat will then consist of three eighth notes.

Remember...
Practise this tune for several days – and only go on to the next page when you feel you're playing it really well. Are you still practising the previous exercises on a regular basis?

Lesson 8 – Strikes, Double High A and Grip

Now you're ready to learn a second tune. It's also a "Slow Air" in 3/4 time – **"Amazing Grace"**. You'll definitely know this melody when you hear it – and that will make learning it easier.

You'll need three new embellishments for this one – the **"Strike, the Double High A and the Grip"**.

Strikes

There are several "Strikes" on very different notes here again, so it really makes sense to learn them all. The strikes are logically organised. First play a melody note, then a G grace note on the middle note of the Strike. Then position your fingers for the third note of the Strike, play it and immediately position your fingers again for the next melody note.

The Bagpipe Tutorial App shows this all very clearly and makes it easy to understand.

The music for the Strike of the melody note D:

"App – Videos – Embellishments – Strikes"

Now write down the **"Strike"** scale in your music book.

Double High A

From any note, first play a short High A, then immediately stroke your left thumb downwards (from top to bottom) over the rear fingerhole to play a G grace note. Make sure that your right (lower) hand finger positioning is correct as you change to the first High A!

The music for the Double High A from the Low A melody note:

"App – Videos – Doublings – Double High A"

Now write down the **"Double High A"** scale in your music book.

Grip (Leumluath)

You have a lot of flexibility with the Grip, because you can play it from any melody note to any melody note. To start with, we'll learn to play it between two identical notes.

1. Play the melody note.

2. Place your fingers on the first Low G position of the Grip.

3. Play a D grace note followed by the second Low G of the Grip.
!!! For the D melody note Grip, play the B grace note instead of the D grace note.

4. Open the fingerhole on the next melody note.

Don't let the first Grip confuse you. The first Low G is missing, because we're already on the Low G melody note. Just play a D grace note followed by the second Low G of the Grip.

The music for the Grip of the melody note High A:

"App – Videos – Embellishments – Grip"

Write down the **"Grip"** scale in your music book.

Now you've got the tool you need to tackle the new tune. Enjoy practising!

"Amazing Grace" is written in 3/4 time. Make sure that you try to count the beat on the quarter note. *Remember that the time value of a grace note and of an embellishment always belongs to the next note. That's why you must play the grace notes and embellishments right on the beat. The Grip is an exception here – start it a little before the beat.*

While you're learning this new tune, it's time to try learning the first part of "Scots Wha Ha'e" by heart.

You should also keep practising your "G-D-E Grace Notes" exercises in **lessons 4 and 5** and your note changing exercises in **lesson 2**.

Remember...
If you practise slowly, you'll become a better piper.
Practice your grace note and embellishment exercises every day if you can.

Amazing Grace   Slow Air   traditional
"App – Videos – Bagpipe Tutorial Tunes"

Now write down the **"Amazing Grace"** tune in your music book.

By now you should also know the names of the notes by heart. Write down the scales in your music book, and write the names of the notes beneath the scales, but from memory!

Are you ready for a very important finger coordination exercise? OK, here we go! First play a Low G then lift each finger briefly, one after the other.

Make sure that you open all your fingers quickly and hold each one at the same distance from the chanter.

Tsunami – Scale
"App – Videos – Single Grace Notes – Tsunami - Scale"

Remember...
At the start, pay special attention to your note changing – it should be very clean with no crossing noises!
Practise your finger exercises and tunes every day if you can.

Lesson 9 – Double B, Double C and the Birl

Now you're ready for your third tune. It's a "March" called the "Highroad to Gairloch" in 2/4 time. Many pipers learn this tune when they start playing the pipes. So it makes sense – even if you can already play this tune – to organise your repertoire in such a way that you can play together with other pipers.

You'll need three new embellishments for this one – **"Double B, Double C and the Birl"**.

Double B

"Doublings" are included among the embellishments. Each note of the scale has a Doubling. You've already learned the first two doublings, "Double HG" and "Double HA". Now we'll focus on the "Double B" and learn how to finger it from every note on the scale.

In the following exercise, first finger the Low G melody note. Now play a G grace note followed by B (the middle note in doubling), a short D grace note and then end on the melody note B. As the name "doubling" implies, it always ends in B.

Repeat this procedure for every note in the scale.

Play a High G melody note, and follow it with a High A grace note instead of the G grace note (also called a thumb grace note). Now play a High G, then briefly lift your left thumb and in the next step close all of your fingers to form a B, followed by the D grace note. We call this doubling the **"Thumb Double B"**.

Here you don't play any G or High A grace notes from the High A melody note just go straight to B then play the D grace note. This doubling is called **"Half Double B"**.

The music for the double B from the Low A melody note:

<u>**"App – Videos – Doublings – Double B"**</u>

Now write down the **"Double B"** scale in your music book.

Then write down the **"Double High G"**, the **"Double High A"** and **"Throw on D"** scales from memory in your music book.

Double C

The "Double C" works in the same way as the "Double B", except that the G and High A grace notes are played from the doubling to the C.
Practise the following scale:

"App – Videos – Doublings – Double C"

Now write down the **"Double C"** scale in your music book.

Birl

The "Birl" is not an easy embellishment to play – you'll need a lot of time to practice it. The most important thing here is keeping your right hand relaxed. There are two ways of fingering the Birl.

Style 1: From the Low A melody note, close the Low G fingerhole with your right pinkie and open it immediately again. Now relax your right pinkie and move it towards your palm to cover the Low G fingerhole. You just heard two short Low Gs!

Style 2: From the Low A melody note, stroke your right pinkie downwards (from top to bottom) over the Low G hole – then move it back up to cover the Low G fingerhole (this is the same as Style 1).

From any other note, a brief Low A must be heard just before the Birl. You can see it in the following "Birl" exercise:

"App – Videos – Embellishments – Birl"

Now write down the **"Birl"** scale in your music book.

Start learning the next tune only when you can play these new embellishments cleanly and confidently. Make sure you play the dotted notes and quarter notes with their correct lengths.

High Road to Gairloch   **March**   **traditional**
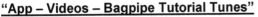

Now write down the **"Highroad to Gairloch"** in your music book.

Lesson 10 – Learning by Heart

We're going to devote an extra lesson to memorising, because it's such an important part of bagpipe music. When you're playing the big bagpipes later, it's important to know the tunes by heart.

OK – now it's time to learn "Scots Wha Ha'e" and "Amazing Grace"... by heart of course!

Listen to the tunes on the **Bagpipe Tutorial App** as often as you can to get them firmly into your ear and memory. This makes it easier to learn them by heart and play them from memory.

Also try to sing or hum along with the tunes with simple "dadadas" or "lalalas". This will give you a better "feeling" for the melody and help you to learn it quickly by heart.

Also look for similar bars and repetitions in the tunes – **if you've identified the tunes' structures, it will be easier for you to memorise them.**

You'll find an interesting lesson on "Learning by Heart" by Dr. Andy Fluck in **lesson 28**.

Lesson 11 – Double E and Double F

Now you're ready for your fourth tune. It's a "March" called **"Mairi's Wedding"** in 2/4 time. This tune is often played as a 2/4 March set together with the "Highroad to Gairloch".

You'll need two new doublings for this one – **"Double E and Double F"**.

Double E

You can play the "Double E" from any note of the scale. Here's how:

1. Play a melody note.

2. Play a G grace note (left index finger) and change to E.

3. Add on an F grace note (left middle finger) and end on the E melody note.

Don't forget that when playing the "Double E" and "Double F" from the High G, we also play a thumb grace note – and from the High A we play a half doubling **(see lesson 9)**.

The music for the double E from the Low A melody note:

<u>**"App – Videos – Doublings – Double E"**</u>

Now write down the **"Double E"** scale in your music book.

Remember...
You can find all these grace notes, the embellishments and the most important exercises summarised in lesson 28. This will save you a lot of page turning when you're performing the individual exercises together with finger technique exercises.

Double F

You can play the "Double F" from any note of the scale. Here's the fingering:

1. Play a melody note.

2. Along with the G grace note (left index finger) change to F.
!!! From a High G melody note, it's a High A grace note (thumb grace note)

3. Play a second G grace note and change to the melody note F.

The music for the double F from the Low A melody note:

"App – Videos – Doublings – Double F"

Now write down the **"Double F"** scale in your music book.

Mairi's Wedding   March   traditional
"App – Videos – Bagpipe Tutorial Tunes"

Now write down **"Mairi's Wedding"** in your music book.

Remember...
Play all the tunes you've learned slowly and cleanly. Your finger technique is paramount – speed will come in time.

Lesson 12 – More Grace Notes and Doublings

Now it's time for us to tackle the rest of the "single grace notes" and "doublings".

Play these embellishments to your tutor as well and let him/her check for any mistakes you might be making. **The Bagpipe Tutorial App** has video and audio recordings that are easy to understand for the following exercises:

F – Grace Note Scale
"App – Videos – Single Grace Notes – F - Grace Note Scale"

Now write down the **"F – Grace Note"** scale in your music book.

High A – Grace Note Scale
"App – Videos – Single Grace Notes – High A - Grace Note Scale"

Now write down the **"High A – Grace Note"** scale in your music book.

Double D
"App – Videos – Doublings – Double D"

Now write down the **"Double D"** scale in your music book.

Double Low A
"App – Videos – Doublings – Double Low A"

Now write down the **"Double Low A"** scale in your music book.

Double Low G
"App – Videos – Doublings – Double Low G"

Now write down the **"Double Low G"** scale in your music book.

The Doubling Scale

Now write down the **"Complete Doubling"** scale in your music book.

Each doubling is played as a half doubling from the High A melody note.

Are you still playing your "G, D, E Grace Note" exercises regularly?

If you practise slowly and play clean note changes, you'll become a better piper.

You'll find a summary of all the Grace Note and Embellishment exercises in lesson 28. Mark the exercises you've already learned to help you identify them quickly – then practise them regularly!

Remember...
Repeat all the technique exercises you've learned as often as possible.
Create a schedule for practising all the exercises and tunes at regular intervals.

OK, now for the fifth tune. It's called **"Brown Haired Maiden"** and is a <u>"March"</u> played in 2/4 time. This tune is another one that you can play with other pipers, because it's popular with pipers all over the world.

If you've repeated all the previous exercises conscientiously, accurately and regularly, the following tune won't be a problem for you – but you probably don't know the melody, so it would be better to listen to it on **the app**.

Brown Haired Maiden   **March**   **traditional**
"App – Videos – Bagpipe Tutorial Tunes"

Now write down **"Brown Haired Maiden"** in your music book.

Remember...
Play all the tunes you've learned very slowly and concentrate on your finger technique.

Lesson 13 – Crossing Noise Exercises

In this lesson you'll learn to change notes cleanly. The following exercises have been designed to help you eliminate imperfections while you're changing notes. Listen closely while you play the following music – are there any slightly imperfect sounds (crossing noises) when you change your fingering?

"App – Videos – Basic Exercises 2 – Crossing Noise Exercise High A - B"

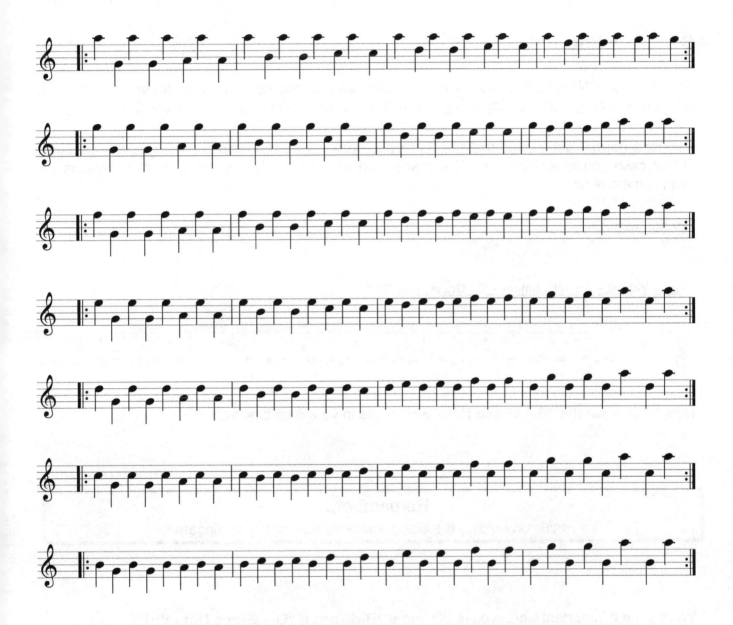

Remember...
Play the note change exercises as often as possible.

Can you already play the first three tunes by heart?

38

Lesson 14 – G – Grace Note Birl

Now you're ready for your sixth tune. It's a "March" called **"Pipes Up"** in 3/4 time.

At this point, our thanks to the composer Ruedi Attinger (Switzerland) for making this tune available for publication in this book.

Before you start, you'll need to learn a new embellishment called the **"G – Grace Note Birl"**.

G – Grace Note Birl

The "G Grace Note Birl" is played in the same way as the normal Birl in **lesson 9**. The only difference here is that you play a G grace note followed by the first Low A of the Birl.

It's just a normal Birl, except that the G – grace note follows the High G melody note – because in this case you're replacing the G – grace note with a High A – grace note which follows the High A melody note.

Try this exercise:

"App – Videos – Embellishment – G - Grace Note Birl"

Now write down the **"G – Grace Note Birl"** scale in your music book.

Remember...
Focus on holding the chanter loosely between your fingers.

What's most important when you're playing a **"Birl"** and a **"G – Grace Note Birl"**?

Do you practice regularly **every day**?

Pipes Up
"App – Videos – Bagpipe Tutorial Tunes"

Now write down **"Pipes Up"** in your music book.

Watch out for rhythmic **"Doublings" and "G Grace Note Birls"**!

By now, you should have learned the first **three tunes** by heart.

What is important when you're playing **"Doublings"**?

Lesson 15 – Rodin

Now you're ready for your seventh tune. It's a "March" called **"The Green Hills of Tyrol"** in 3/4 time.

It is always advisable to learn more and more tunes that have one kind of time signature, since they all have similar characteristics and emphases.

This will enable you to compile and play a set of several songs with the same time signature.

Before you start, you'll need a new embellishment called the **"Rodin"**.

Rodin

This is very similar to the "Grip".

1. Play a melody note.

2. Place all your fingers in the Low G position.

3. Play a B grace note (right ring finger) followed by a Low G.

4. Now open your fingers to play the Low A melody note.

The music for the Rodin of the C melody note:

"App – Videos – Embellishment – Rodin"

Now write down the **"Rodin"** exercise in your music book.

The Green Hills of Tyrol   **Retreat March**   **traditional**
"App – Videos – Bagpipe Tutorial Tunes"

Write down **"The Green Hills of Tyrol"** in your music book.

Lesson 16 – Right and Wrong Habits

1) Always hold the practice chanter loosely in your fingers – don't tighten up! Playing the different embellishments and the notes is much more strenuous if your fingers are cramped.

2) Always make sure your fingers are lying straight, stretched and relaxed.

3) If you're sitting, always sit straight with your back as close as possible to the chair back and your knees bent at a 90° angle. Let your elbows hang loose and relaxed at your sides.

4) Try to hold the practice chanter pointing diagonally downward. If possible, avoid laying it on the table – while you're playing, hold it in the air without any other contact (apart from your hands of course!).

5) When you're playing the embellishments, all your notes should be of the same length and easily audible. Don't get careless. Your objective should always be a clean and rhythmic finger technique.

6) Have you written all the tunes and exercises into your music book? If you've missed one or two, write them in there now. That's really important!

7) Practice every day, as often and as long as possible. Regular practice is crucial.

8) Play the tunes and the exercises you've learned regularly. These are the "heart of your art". The more accurately you practice your embellishments, the cleaner and faster you'll play your tunes.

9) OK, you have this textbook and the instructional Bagpipe Tutor App – but I really recommend that you look for a tutor. He or she can listen to you playing your exercises and tunes and correct any errors that might have crept in.

10) Visit workshops to learn even more and meet other pipers. This will also increase your motivation to practice every day.

Write down all the **"Doubling Scales"** in your music book – <u>but from memory</u>!

Are you practising your embellishment exercises every day?

Remember...
While playing, lift your fingers up just far enough to generate clear, clean tones.
Finger your embellishments openly and evenly.

Lesson 17 – Revision

> ➢ Can you remember what's really important when you're playing the **"Throw on D"** and the **"Grip"**?

> ➢ Which time signature does "Amazing Grace" have? Can you beat the correct time to the song with your foot or the metronome, <u>just from memory</u>?

> ➢ What is a **3/4 bar**? What characteristics does it have?

> ➢ Can you write down the **"Double D"** and **"Double High G"** scales <u>from memory</u> in your music book?

> ➢ What do you have to watch when a **"Grip"** follows a D melody note?

> ➢ In the case of the **"Birl"**, what do you have to watch out for when you play the first Low A in the embellishment?

> ➢ What's more effective? Practising once a week for four hours or every day for 30 minutes?

> ➢ Can you play **"Pipes Up"** from memory?

> ➢ What's a **"Crossing Noise"** and can you identify it if you hear it?

> ➢ What's a really important thing to remember if you want to become a good piper?

> ➢ **Where does your motivation come from?**

Lesson 18 – The Taorluath and Revision of the Grip

This is your eighth tune. It's a <u>"March"</u> called **"Scotland the Brave"** in 4/4 time.

This is a well-known piece and is also one of the anthems of Scotland.

Scotland the Brave is classed as one of the more difficult tunes to learn because of its many embellishments.

Try to learn the tune slowly and conscientiously, don't rush it. Play all the embellishments cleanly and pay attention that your rhythm is correct (with this tune, it's best to use the metronome to make sure you're playing the note values with their correct lengths).

Before we start, let's learn the **"Taorluath"**.

Taorluath

This is very similar to the "Grip" (Leumluath).

1. Play a G grace note followed by a melody note.

2. Place your fingers on the first Low G position of the Taorluath.

3. Play a D grace note followed by the second Low G of the Taorluath.
!!! To play the Taorluath after a D melody note, replace the D grace note with a B grace note.

4. Now play an E grace note followed by the next melody note.

The music for the Low A melody note Taorluath:

"App – Videos – Embellishment – Taorluath"

Now write down the **"Taorluath"** exercise in your music book.

"App – Videos – Embellishment – Taorluath on Low A"

Now write down the **"Taorluath"** scale in your music book.

Repeat the **"Grip"** (Leumluath) to practice both embellishments intensively.

Grip

"App – Videos – Embellishment – Grip"

Here are three more Grip exercises.

Grip Scale, Upper Hand

Grip Scale, Lower Hand

Grip Scale, Full

Now write down the **"Grip"** exercises in your music book.

Remember...
Focus on changing your fingers cleanly from the Grip's second Low G to the next melody note – this is where crossing noises are most likely to occur.

Scotland the Brave   March   traditional
"App – Videos – Bagpipe Tutorial Tunes"

Now write down **"Scotland the Brave"** in your music book.

Now you should be able to play the first four tunes accurately and cleanly – <u>from memory</u>.

Lesson 19 – Rhythm / Monotone Exercises

The table below shows you the most common time signatures. Here you can see exactly what possibilities there are to structure a bar and the different rhythms you can create from that.

The arrow indicates that the beat (foot/metronome) falls on that particular note (or on the previous embellishment).

The small X represents the offbeat. On the offbeat, your foot should always be in the air.

Lesson 20 – G-D-E Single Grace Note Jumps

Play the following exercises slowly and cleanly. Change fingers cleanly, avoiding "crossing noises".

Practice these exercises for a few days, and then play them through several times as often as you can.

!!! Here you have to change the tone with the D grace note.

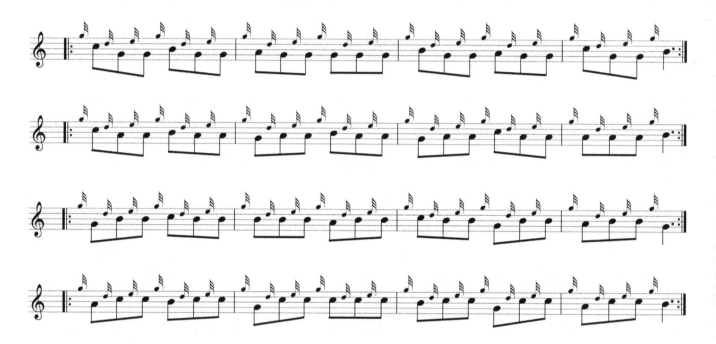

Now repeat the G-D-E technique exercises in **lesson 5**.

Remember...

These G-D-E jumps are essential exercises. Even the best pipers in the world regularly play them and the other exercises of the previous lessons.

To use these note combinations in a tune, we'll now learn a four-part "<u>Jig</u>" called **"Paddy's Leather Breeches"** written in 6/8.

Paddy's Leather Breeches   Jig   traditional
"App – Videos – Bagpipe Tutorial Tunes"

Now write down **"Paddy's Leather Breeches"** in your music book.

Again, try to learn it slowly and conscientiously, don't rush it. Make sure that you play the G-D-E grace notes evenly.

Only start the next lesson if you can already play the first five tunes <u>from memory</u>!

     48

Lesson 21 – The Set of Bagpipes

You've now learned nine tunes, lots of exercises and most of the embellishments for the Highland Bagpipe. Now I suggest you buy a set of bagpipes in the shop of your choice – but before you decide on a particular set, get as much advice as possible from the professional sales person there. This is important, because the pipes you buy will probably accompany you your whole life long, so **choose wisely**.

Make sure you're being offered good accessories too, like a carrying case, brushes, oil, cleaning products, the right bag size plus any other accessory materials you might need.

When you finally have brought your pipes home with you, start working with this textbook again **from scratch**. This time, you'll be using your own bagpipes instead of the practice chanter. You can still use the chanter for practising your exercises and tunes – **and also for the next lesson, which is number 22**.

Here is an overview of the various parts of a set of bagpipes.

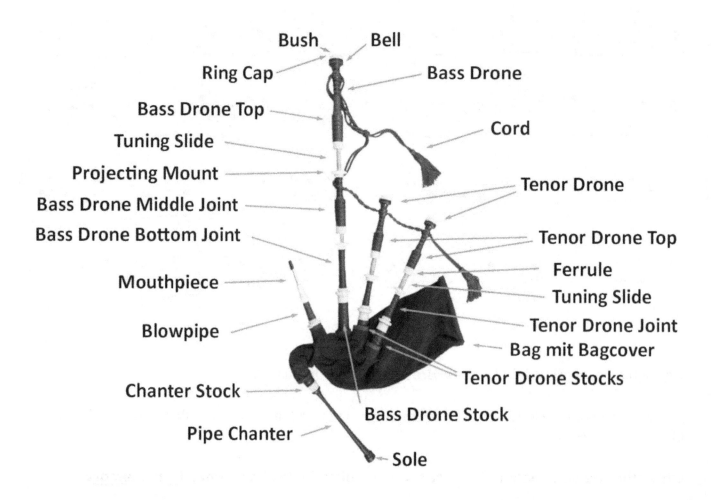

Lesson 22 – Strathspey Triplets

Now you're ready for your tenth tune. It's a "Strathspey" called **"Aspen Bank"** in 4/4 time.

I can almost hear you asking, "What the heck is a "Strathspey"? The answer is that it's a region in Scotland after which this type of dance tune is named.

Once again, try to learn the tune slowly and conscientiously, don't rush it. Play all the embellishments cleanly and make sure you've got the right rhythm. There are four beats to the bar.

The special feature of Strathspeys is the very strong emphasis on some notes – so emphasise the dotted notes strongly and make the short sixteenth notes very short.

Many pipers claim that the first and third beats in the bar have to be emphasised more than the other two in a Strathspey. You could try that as well.

But before you start, you'll need a new exercise, the **"Strathspey Triplets"**.

Strathspey Triplets

These triplets are played very fast and end with the third and longest note.

Remember that the beat is always on the first note of the triplet, but the emphasis is still on the third and final note.

"App – Videos – More Exercises – Strathspey Triplets"

Now write down the **"Triplet"** scale in your music book.

Remember...
Speed isn't your main priority here. Play all the exercises slowly and cleanly.
Play the tunes musically and focus strongly on rhythm and intonation.

Aspen Bank   **Strathspey**   **traditional**
"App – Videos – Bagpipe Tutorial Tunes"

Now write down **"Aspen Bank"** in your music book.

Lesson 23 – Tachum, Double Tachum and Darado

Your eleventh tune is another "Strathspey", called **"Devil in the Kitchen"** in 4/4 time.

You have three new embellishments to learn for this one – the **"Tachum"**, the **"Double Tachum"** and the **"Darado"**.

Tachums

This is a combination of notes that occurs very frequently in the more challenging tunes.

This particular combination consists of a G grace note followed by a very short melody note, which in turn is followed by a D grace note and the next dotted melody note.

"App – Videos – Embellishments – Tachums"

Write down the **"Tachum"** exercise in your music book.

"App – Videos – More Exercises – D - Grace Note Tachum Variation"

Practise the Tachum exercises slowly and cleanly. Make sure that the grace notes are played exactly on the notes that follow – don't let any crossing noises creep in!

Double Tachums

The Double Tachum consists of a Doubling and an E grace note followed by a deeper melody note. This sequence must result in a triplet rhythm. Here I really recommend that you take a look at the relevant video on the **app**.

"App – Videos – Embellishments – Double Tachums"

Now write down the **"Double Tachum"** exercise in your music book.

"App – Videos – More Exercises – Strathspey Double Tachums 1"

Write down the **"Taorluath on Low A"** scale <u>from memory</u> in your music book.

Write down the **"Grip"** scale in your music book, <u>also from memory</u>.

Darado – Bubbly Note

The "Darado" is an embellishment you won't come across very often – and that's why it's important to practice it as often as you can, because there's nothing worse for a piper than being confronted with a piece you don't know!

1. Play a melody note.

2. Place all your fingers in a Low G position.

3. Play a D grace note followed by a Low G.

4. Play a C grace note with your right middle finger followed by a Low G.

5. Follow this with a B melody note.

The music for the Darado of the B melody note:

"App – Videos – Embellishments – Darado - Bubbly Note"

Now write down the **"Darado"** exercise in your music book.

Devil in the Kitchen   Strathspey   traditional
"App – Videos – Bagpipe Tutorial Tunes"

Now write down **"Devil in the Kitchen"** in your music book.

We're going to learn **"Devil in the Kitchen"** again, but this time as a <u>Reel</u> and not a Strathspey. A Reel is a dance song and is always written in 2/2 (Alla Breve-Timing). Although we have four quarter notes per bar, you only beat (with your foot) on the half beat.

Devil in the Kitchen   Reel   traditional
"App – Videos – Bagpipe Tutorial Tunes"

Now write down **"Devil in the Kitchen"** in your music book.

Remember...
Strathspeys and Reels are played at a higher speed. However, the finger technique is paramount. Speed will come with practice and time.

Here's a beautiful tune for you.

Morag of Dunvegan   Slow Air   traditional
"App – Videos – Bagpipe Tutorial Tunes"

Lesson 24 – Fast Finger Exercise

Now you'll learn how to change notes faster. Try these exercises – they will help you to develop faster and more controlled fingering.

Start slowly and increase the speed of the demi-semi quavers (the very short 1/32 notes).

"App – Videos – More Exercises – Fast Finger Exercise High A - B"

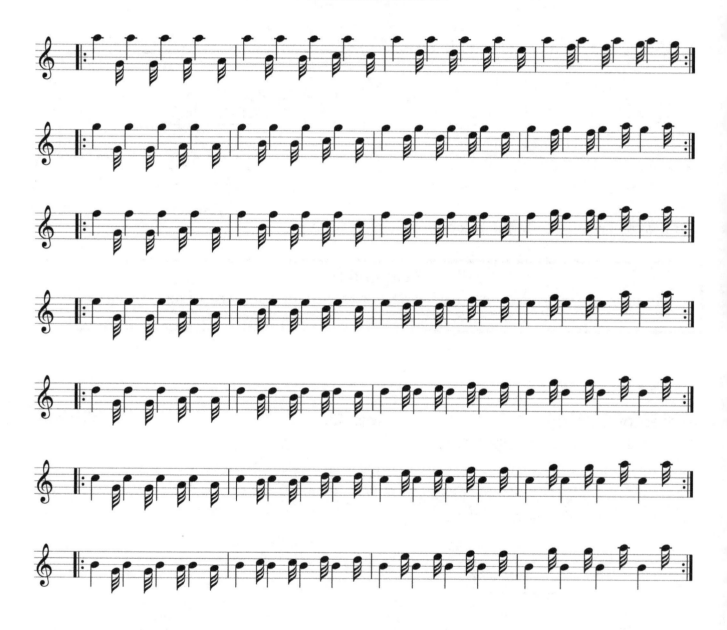

Are you still practising all the Doublings and Single Grace Notes?

Try not to neglect these exercises. Then you can transfer them gradually to your set of bagpipes.

Lesson 25 – Music Theory

So far, you've learned quite a few bagpipe music time signatures – but there are others too and they all have different characteristics.

Here is an overview of the most important time signatures.

Tune type	Type of time signature	Beats per bar	Emphasis on the beats	Revision?
Slow Air	6/8 / 2/4 / 3/4 etc.	Dep. on the time signature	Dep. on the time signature	Dep. on the time signature
2/4 March	2/4	Two	Strong – medium	Yes
3/4 March	3/4	Three	Strong – medium – medium	Yes
4/4 March	4/4	Four	Strong – medium – medium – medium	No
6/8 March	6/8	Two	Strong – medium	Yes
9/8 March	9/8	Three	Strong – medium – medium	Yes
12/8 March	12/8	Four	Strong – medium – medium – medium	Yes
Strathspey	4/4	Four	Very strong – medium – medium – medium	No
Reel	2/2	Two	Strong – medium	No
Hornpipe	2/4	Two	Strong – medium	Yes
Jig	6/8 – 9/8	two	Each 1st 8th note is emphasised a little	Yes

Simple Time (even time signatures)   **2/4 – 3/4 – 4/4 – 2/2**

Compound Time (odd time signatures)   **6/8 – 9/8 – 12/8**

How many 1/8 notes = 1/4 note? ___   How many 1/4 notes = 1/2 note? ___

How many 1/2 notes = two whole notes? ___   Draw a 1/8 note: ___

How many 1/16 notes = 1/8 note? ___   Draw a whole note: ___

How many 1/32 notes = two 1/16 notes? ___

Draw the repeat signs: _____   Draw a G grace note: ___

How many 1/16 notes are in one bar of a 6/8 Tune? ___

Lesson 26 – More Exercises and Embellishments

The following exercise will help you to really improve your "Double Tachums" and your "G-D-E triplets". Listen to the recording on the **app** and try to practise the exercise as regularly as possible.

Strathspey Double Tachums and Triplets
"App – Videos – More Exercises – Strathspey Double Tachums 2"

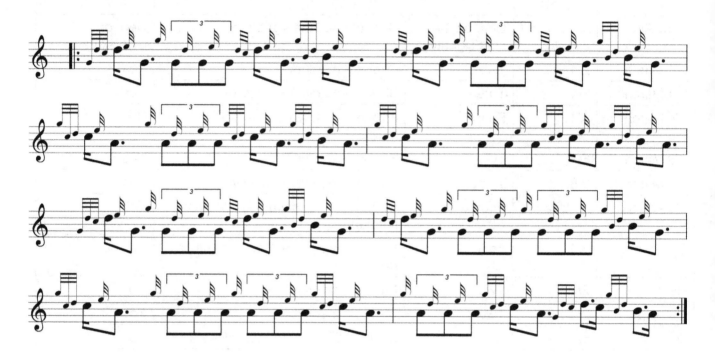

Remember...
The exercises in **lessons 5, 18, 20, 23** and **26** are very important. Even advanced pipers should practise them regularly.
Try to repeat all the technique exercises you've learned at regular intervals.

I haven't included the following two embellishments **"Double Catch on B"** and **"Double Catch on C"** in the book until now, because these two rarely occur in bagpipe music – but you should practise them anyway, because you might need them at some time or other.

They are very similar to the Grip, so they won't be too difficult for you to learn.

Double Catch on B

1. Play a melody note.

2. Now play a short B.

3. Place your fingers on the Low G position.

4. Now play a short D grace note followed by the second Low G.

5. Follow this with a B melody note.

"App – Videos – Embellishments – Double Catch on B"

Now write down the **"Double Catch on B"** exercise in your music book.

Double Catch on C

1. Play a melody note.

2. Now play a short C.

3. Place your fingers on the Low G position.

4. Now play a short D grace note followed by the second Low G.

5. Follow this with a C melody note.

"App – Videos – Embellishments – Double Catch on C"

Now write down the **"Double Catch on C"** exercise in your music book.

Double Strikes

This embellishment occurs most often in Hornpipe tunes, but you haven't learned the Hornpipe yet. Ask your tutor about the Hornpipe – he or she will probably give you an exercise or two to practice this embellishment. The Hornpipe is only played on the B, C and D melody notes:

1. Play the relevant melody note.

2. Play a G grace note followed by the second note in the Double Strike.

3. Play an E grace note followed by the fourth note in the Double Strike.

4. Play a short Low G followed by the final note.

<u>**"App – Videos – Embellishments – Double Strikes"**</u>

Now write down the **"Double Strike"** exercise in your music book.

Congratulations! So far you've learned thirteen tunes (yes, 13!) and the most important embellishments for playing the pipes.

Now you have the tools to learn even more tunes. Your specialist dealer very probably has great books of tunes like **"Scots Guards"** or the **"Donald MacLeod Collection"** in stock. These books have plenty of tunes to expand your repertoire.

If you're uncertain about technicalities or if you have questions about new tunes, you can always rely on this textbook and the accompanying **app** to help you out.

Yet another music style is the old **"Classic"** bagpipe music, the **"Piobaireachd"**.

If you want to take your first steps in "Piobaireachd", I strongly advise you to consult a teacher who will start you on your journey into the world of the old bagpipe music and explain how best to proceed.

Lesson 28 has all the Piobaireachd embellishments you'll ever need.

The relevant videos are in the **Bagpipe Tutorial App in the Piobaireachd section**.

Take a look at the tunes in the next lesson, you might just find them interesting. And all the best with your bagpipe playing! Enjoy your instrument!

Lesson 27 – More Tunes

I wrote this tune for my son Kevin. It's about all the good times we've been able to spend together.

Kevin's Tune   **Slow Air**   **Andreas Hambsch**
"App – Videos – Bagpipe Tutorial Tunes"

Jock Wilson's Ball   **Reel**   **tradition**
"App – Videos – Bagpipe Tutorial Tunes"

The Mermaid Song   Slow Air   traditional
"App – Videos – Bagpipe Tutorial Tunes"

Orange and Blue   Strathspey   traditional
"App – Videos – Bagpipe Tutorial Tunes"

The High Road To Linton   Reel   tradition
"App – Videos – Bagpipe Tutorial Tunes"

The Skye Boat Song   Slow Air   tradition
"App – Videos – Bagpipe Tutorial Tunes"

Heather Island   Slow Air   traditional
"App – Videos – Bagpipe Tutorial Tunes"

The following tune is dedicated to the memory of Pipe Major Joe Wilson. He was – and still remains even after his death – a true luminary in the world of piping.

Many thanks to the composer Dr. Christian Grosser for making this tune,
"P.M. Joe Wilson's Welcome to the College of Piping" available for publication in this book.

P.M. Joe Wilson was our mutual friend and teacher for many years. He was a fantastically-skilled piper and a true gentleman.

P.M. Joe Wilson's Welcome to the C.o.P.   March
"App – Videos – Bagpipe Tutorial Tunes"

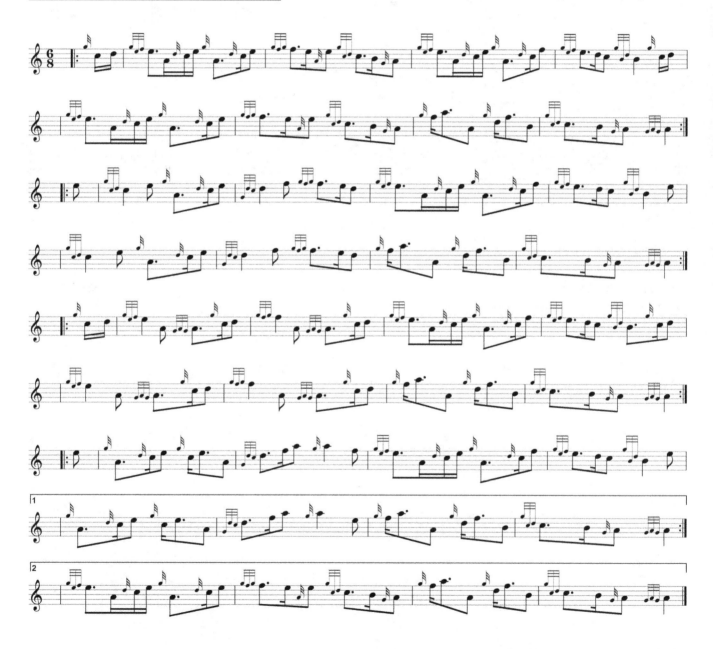

Happy Birthday   **Slow Air**   **traditional**
"App – Videos – Bagpipe Tutorial Tunes"

Acknowledgements

Many people have accompanied me on my path to becoming a bagpipe teacher and tutor. I would like to especially thank the following people for their constant and unselfish help:

My family and friends who encouraged me to learn this instrument at a young age and who are still a great support for me today.

My sister Heidi Mayer, who produced the Videos and created the graphics.

All my tutors who have taught me over the years. Every one of them was and still is a great role model for me.

My students who enable me to carry out my profession as a bagpipe tutor by participating in my classes.

All the bands and organisations that regularly invite me to their workshops.

All the dealers who support me by selling my teaching materials.

I'm grateful to have met these people and I'm looking forward to meeting many more interesting people in my life as a bagpiper

I wish you lots of enjoyment with your bagpipes and I sincerely hope that you will always find new motivation to play your instrument.

It's a wonderful thing if you can bring beautiful music to the world and touch other people with it.

Lesson 28 – Grace Notes, Embellishments and Exercises

App - Video - Basic Exercises 1 - Low G to Low A Scale

App - Video - Basic Exercises 1 - Low G to B Scale

App - Video - Basic Exercises 1 - Low G to C Scale

App - Video - Basic Exercises 1 - Low G to C Exercise

App - Video - Basic Exercises 1 - Low G to D Scale

App - Video - Basic Exercises 1 - Low G to D Exercise

App - Video - Basic Exercises 1 - Low G to E Scale

App - Video - Basic Exercises 1 - Low G to E Exercise

App - Video - Basic Exercises 1 - D to E Exercise

App - Video - Basic Exercises 1 - Low G to F Scale

App - Video - Basic Exercises 1 - Low G to F Exercise

App - Video - Basic Exercises 1 - Low G to High G Scale

App - Video - Basic Exercises 1 - Low G to High G Exercise

App - Video - Basic Exercises 1 - Low G to High A Scale

App - Video - Basic Exercises 1 - Low G to High A Exercise

App - Videos - Basic Exercises 2 - Changing Exercise 1

App - Videos - Basic Exercises 2 - Changing Exercise 2

App - Videos - Basic Exercises 2 - Changing Exercise 3

App - Videos - Basic Exercises 2 - Changing Exercise 4

App - Videos - Basic Exercises 2 - Changing Exercise 5

App - Videos - Basic Exercises 2 - Changing Exercise 6

App - Videos - Basic Exercises 2 - Changing Exercise 7

App - Basic Exercises 2 - Crossing Noise Exercise High A

App - Basic Exercises 2 - Crossing Noise Exercise High G

App - Basic Exercises 2 - Crossing Noise Exercise F

App - Basic Exercises 2 - Crossing Noise Exercise E

App - Basic Exercises 2 - Crossing Noise Exercise D

App - Basic Exercises 2 - Crossing Noise Exercise C

App - Basic Exercises 2 - Crossing Noise Exercise B

App - Basic Exercises 2 - Crossing Noise Exercise Low A

App - Videos - Single Grace Notes - D - Grace Note Scale

App - Videos - Single Grace Notes - E - Grace Note Scale

App - Videos - Single Grace Notes - F - Grace Note Scale

App - Videos - Single Grace Notes - High G - Grace Note Scale

App - Videos - Single Grace Notes - High A - Grace Note Scale

App - Videos - Single Grace Notes - Tsunami - Scale

App - Videos - Single Grace Notes - G-D-E Exercise 1

App - Videos - Single Grace Notes - G-D-E Exercise 2

App - Videos - Single Grace Notes - G-D-E Exercise 3

App - Videos - Single Grace Notes - G-D-E Exercise 4

App - Videos - Single Grace Notes - G-D-E Exercise 5

Lesson 20 - G-D-E Single Grace Note Jumps to Low G

Lesson 20 - G-D-E Single Grace Note Jumps to Low A

Lesson 20 - G-D-E Single Grace Note Jumps to B

Lesson 20 - G-D-E Single Grace Note Jumps to C

Additional G-D-E Jumps

Additional G-D-E Jumps

Additional G-D-E Jumps

App - Videos - Doublings - Double High A

App - Videos - Doublings - Double High G

App - Videos - Doublings - Double F

App - Videos - Doublings - Double E

App - Videos - Doublings - Double D

App - Videos - Doublings - Double C

App - Videos - Doublings - Double B

App - Videos - Doublings - Double Low A

App - Videos - Doublings - Double Low G

Doubling Scale

"How i memorise a song" by Dr. Andy Fluck

1. Look at the notes and "feel" how *great* it's going to be playing this interesting tune from memory. If you can, listen to the tune beforehand as often as possible and sing along with it as best you can.

2. The piece is already divided into parts. Sub-divide these parts into phrases. A phrase (almost) always consists of two bars (possibly with an intro). Go through the tune and see where some phrases are repeated. Pay attention to the individual parts' intros – parts 1 and 3 and parts 2 and 4 are often identical.

3. Learn the first phrase by heart. Play it from memory. Learn the second phrase by heart. Play it from memory. Play the first and second phrases from memory, one after the other. If you can't remember how it goes at one particular point in the tune, <u>only look at that one note you've forgotten</u> (you know the rest by heart anyway).

4. Learn the third phrase by heart. Play it from memory. Play the first, second and third phrases from memory. If you can't remember how it goes at one particular point in the tune... etc. Work your way through the first part like this, playing it from memory.

5. Work your way through the second part in the same way. Play it from memory. Now play the first and second parts from memory, then the third part from memory. Now repeat the first three parts several times from memory. OK, it's time for the fourth part now.

6. First, second, third and fourth.
!!! The golden rule here is that if you forget one or two notes anywhere in the tune, <u>only look at these particular notes in the music</u> – do NOT look at the rest of the piece.

7. It's "feelgood" time now! Look how quickly you've learned the tune by heart! And if a couple of notes were missing, so what? They're easily learned :-).

8. I can't stress enough how really important points 1 and 7 are here. In point 1, if you don't really believe that it's going to work, you'll find that learning the single notes in 3-6 will be a disaster – and this will just strengthen your unconscious and unproductive non-belief in yourself and in this method, because you'll start thinking **"I can't do this anyway"**. But if you really try to "<u>feel</u>" how great it's going to be playing the tune from memory, you'll be delighted with everything you were able to remember – and when you forget a note or two, you'll simply say, **"That's OK, it happens!"**. So when you read points 1 and 7, please DON'T underestimate how psychologically important they are for learning a tune by heart!

Andy Fluck

App - Videos - Embellishments - Throw on D Style 1

App - Videos - Embellishments - Throw on D Style 2

App - Videos - Embellishments - Grip

App - Videos - Embellishments - Double Catch on B

App - Videos - Embellishments - Double Catch on C

App - Videos - Embellishments - Taorluath

App - Videos - Embellishments - Taorluath on Low A

App - Videos - Embellishments - Birl

App - Videos - Embellishments - G - Grace Note Birl

App - Videos - Embellishments - Half Strikes

App - Videos - Embellishments - Strikes

App - Videos - Embellishments - Double Strikes

App - Videos - Embellishments - Tachums

App - Videos - Embellishments - Double Tachums

App - Videos - Embellishments - Rodin

App - Videos - Embellishments - Darado - Bubbly Note

App - Videos - Piobaireachd - Taorluath Amach

App - Videos - Piobaireachd - Crunluath

App - Videos - Piobaireachd - Crunluath Breabach

App - Videos - Piobaireachd - Crunluath Amach

App - Videos - Piobaireachd - Crunluath Fosgailte

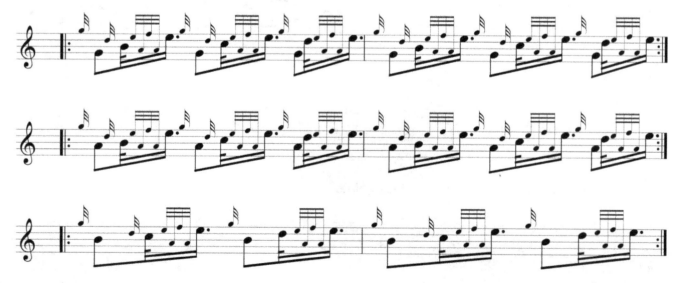

App - Videos - Piobaireachd - Dre

App - Videos - Piobaireachd - Dare

App - Videos - Piobaireachd - Chedare

App - Videos - Piobaireachd - Bari

App - Videos - Piobaireachd - Adeda

App - Videos - Piobaireachd - Harin

App - Videos - Piobaireachd - Double Echos

App - Videos - More Exercises - Strathspey Triplets

App - Videos - More Exercises - 6/8-Movements

App - Videos - More Exercises - Strathspey Double Tachums 1

App - Videos - More Exercises - Strathspey Double Tachums 2

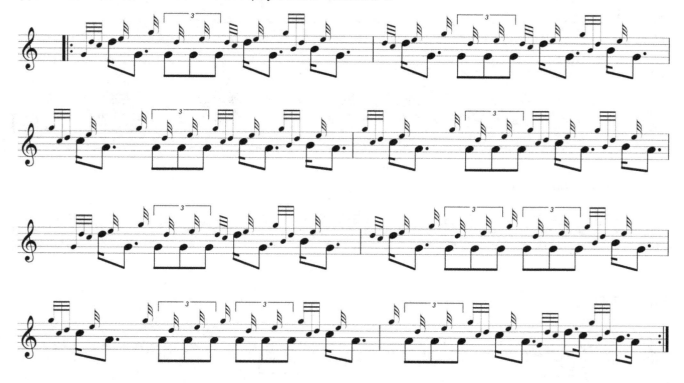

App - Videos - More Exercises - D - Grace Note Tachum Variation

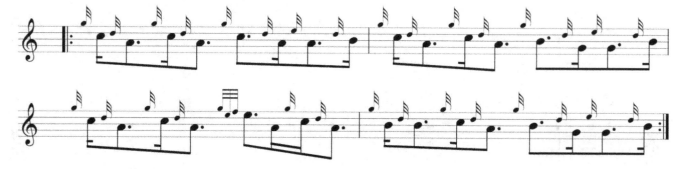

App - Videos - More Exercises - Fast Finger Exercise High A

App - Videos - More Exercises - Fast Finger Exercise High G

App - Videos - More Exercises - Fast Finger Exercise F

App - Videos - More Exercises - Fast Finger Exercise E

App - Videos - More Exercises - Fast Finger Exercise D

App - Videos - More Exercises - Fast Finger Exercise C

App - Videos - More Exercises - Fast Finger Exercise B

App - Videos - More Exercises - Fast Finger Exercise Low A

App - Videos - More Exercises - Fast Finger Exercise Low G

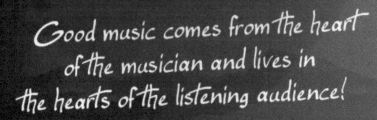

Good music comes from the heart of the musician and lives in the hearts of the listening audience!

ANDREAS HAMBSCH
PROFESSIONAL BAGPIPE INSTRUCTOR

ABOUT THE AUTHOR

Andreas Hambsch, professional bagpipe instructor, began playing the bagpipes in 1993. He has won many high-profile solo competitions and for some years was also a member of a Scottish Grade 1 professional pipe band, competing against the best pipe bands in the world.

In 2007, he completed his teacher's examination at the Scottish College of Piping and received the college's highest diploma in the art of bagpipe playing in 2010. He then opened a bagpipe school and since then has worked as a full-time teacher tutoring students from all over the world.

Andreas Hambsch also hosts band workshops, teaches at international summer and winter schools and makes a major contribution towards making Scottish music better known all over the world. Thanks to his musical and social skills as a bagpipe teacher, he is very popular with his students and his services as a teacher are very much in demand.

This book by Andreas Hambsch marks a milestone in the teaching of the Scottish bagpipes. It is a professional educational tool to help you learn how to play and understand the bagpipes. Beginners and advanced players can achieve rapid success.